FORGOTTEN KINGS AND KINGDOMS

Robyn Hardyman

raintree
a Capstone company — publishers for children

Raintree is an imprint of Capstone Global Library Limited, a company incorporated in England and Wales having its registered office at 264 Banbury Road, Oxford, OX2 7DY – Registered company number: 6695582

www.raintree.co.uk
myorders@raintree.co.uk

Text © Capstone Global Library Limited 2021
The moral rights of the proprietor have been asserted.

All rights reserved. No part of this publication may be reproduced in any form or by any means (including photocopying or storing it in any medium by electronic means and whether or not transiently or incidentally to some other use of this publication) without the written permission of the copyright owner, except in accordance with the provisions of the Copyright, Designs and Patents Act 1988 or under the terms of a licence issued by the Copyright Licensing Agency, Barnard's Inn, 86 Fetter Lane, London, EC4A 1EN (www.cla.co.uk). Applications for the copyright owner's written permission should be addressed to the publisher.

Produced for Raintree by Calcium
Edited by Sarah Eason and Claudia Martin
Designed by Emma DeBanks
Original illustrations © Capstone Global Library Limited 2021
Media research by Rachel Blount
Printed and bound in the United Kingdom

978 1 3982 0071 5 (hardback)
978 1 3982 0094 4 (paperback)

British Library Cataloguing in Publication Data
A full catalogue record for this book is available from the British Library.

Acknowledgements
We would like to thank the following for permission to reproduce photographs: ChiccoDodiFC br, Bill Frische tr, Larisa Koshkina bg, Nejron Photo bl, Vadim Petrakov r; Inside: Shutterstock: 2630ben 12b, Paulo Afonso 21t, Akiyoko 40–41bg, Galyna Andrushko 14–15bg, Antb 34–35bg, Anton_Ivanov 4–5bg, Atiger 38–39bg, B Studio 26–27bg, Klaus Balzano 20b, Jim Barber 42–43bg, Filip Bjorkman 25b, Borna_Mirahmadian 30b, 31t, Bulent Camci 6–7bg, Dmitry Chulov 11b, Everett – Art 35, 39t, 40l, 42b, Gordon Galbraith 16, Fer Gregory 14b, 32b, Helen Hotson 32–33bg, Irisphoto1 37, Andreas Juergensmeier 34b, Tomaz Kunst 20–21bg, M.V. Photography 16–17bg, 17, Meliksetyan Marianna 27r, Martchan 10–11bg, Mikadun 8–9bg, Luciano Mortula 24–25bg, Muratart 26b, Lenar Musin 5r, Ollirg 22–23bg, Optimarc 12–13bg, Pecold 6b, Perfect Lazybones 29r, Maxim Petrichuk 30–31bg, Radiokafka 10b, Leon Rafael 15t, Matyas Rehak 19, Aleksei Sarkisov 28t, Lena Serditova 28–29bg, Valdis Skudre 36–37bg, Sergey Uryadnikov 18–19bg, Vanille 8b, Yolka 18; Wikimedia Commons: James Archer, 1860 36, Julia Margaret Cameron, Royal Photographic Society 33t, Samuel Cousins (died 1887), after Sir John Everett Millais (original 1878) 38b, Gift of Ruth and Milton Hecht 25t, Sue Hutton 41, Alexander Kucharsky 43t, Matt Neale from UK 13t, Marie-Lan Nguyen 9t, © Manuel González Olaechea y Franco 7, Philip Pikart 23, Klaus-Peter Simon 22b.

Every effort has been made to contact copyright holders of material reproduced in this book. Any omissions will be rectified in subsequent printings if notice is given to the publisher.

All the internet addresses (URLs) given in this book were valid at the time of going to press. However, due to the dynamic nature of the internet, some addresses may have changed, or sites may have changed or ceased to exist since publication. While the author and publisher regret any inconvenience this may cause readers, no responsibility for any such changes can be accepted by either the author or the publisher.

CONTENTS

Chapter 1
Lost kings and kingdoms 4

Chapter 2
Lost kingdoms of Africa 8

Chapter 3
Lost kingdoms of the Americas 14

Chapter 4
Great lost empires and their rulers 22

Chapter 5
King Arthur 32

Chapter 6
What happened to them? 38

Mystery hunter answers 44
Glossary 46
Find out more 47
Index 48

Chapter 1
LOST KINGS AND KINGDOMS

The modern world is mainly comprised of nations, or countries, each with a government and a leader. Their systems of government are varied. Some countries are monarchies, with a king or queen who inherits his or her role as **head of state**. In other countries, the head of state is the president, who is elected. In many countries, called democracies, people take an active part in how they are governed. It may seem as if this pattern has been around forever, but a look back into history reveals that this is not the case.

Rise and fall

For several thousand years, since people first settled into farming communities that grew into cities and, later, countries, the borders between peoples have been on the move. The fortunes of different regions have also changed. A place that was once mighty, such as ancient Egypt, for example, may today be a much less powerful player in the world.

The power of once-mighty kingdoms such as ancient Egypt fades away over time.

Some remarkably powerful kingdoms have appeared – and disappeared. It is a familiar pattern: a kingdom gets bigger, with more influence over its neighbours. It enjoys a period of greatness, then it is gone. Sometimes the end is sudden, if a kingdom is overrun by an enemy. Sometimes the **decline** is more gradual, as the situation in a region changes. For a kingdom to rise to greatness, it needs a powerful ruler: a man or woman with vision and determination. The stories of these kingdoms and their rulers are fascinating. They remind us that things change, and that the powerful countries of today may not be the powers of tomorrow.

Clues to the past

Over time, we have lost sight of many of the great kingdoms and **empires** of the past. They have become a mystery to us. We can look at some of the clues they have left behind to solve their mysteries and wonder at their achievements.

The city of Angkor, Cambodia, was once the centre of an empire. It fell into decay and was lost in the jungle.

MYSTERY HUNTER

Look for the mystery hunter boxes throughout the book. They will ask you to consider the information given in each chapter and answer questions based on what you have read. Then turn to pages 44–45 to see if your answers are correct.

Solving the mysteries

How can we find out about these mysteries from the past? We need clues, of course. Sometimes lost kingdoms leave behind **evidence**, such as ruined buildings and **artefacts**, or objects. All kinds of people work to unlock these mysteries for us.

Finding a lost queen

Over time, abandoned buildings fall into ruin, and their stones may be hidden under layers of earth. **Archaeologists** are some of the best mystery hunters around. Their job is to find places where there might possibly be clues to the past, and to dig! They have to work slowly and carefully, so they do not destroy any evidence, but they have made most of the amazing discoveries of the last few hundred years, solving the mysteries of many lost kingdoms. One of their great discoveries was about the Egyptian queen Hatshepsut, who ruled in about 1473 BC. She ordered the building of many magnificent temples, but after her death the next **pharaoh** tried to remove all trace of her. He destroyed or spoiled her monuments and erased her **inscriptions**, so we knew very little about her. Little by little, archaeologists have uncovered evidence about this mysterious queen.

We are still finding out the secrets of Queen Hatshepsut.

This is a reconstruction of what the Moche woman in the pyramid may have looked like.

Mysterious Moche

In 2006, archaeologists in northern Peru were working deep inside a mud-brick pyramid. They were amazed to find the perfectly preserved body of a young woman who had died 1,500 years before. Buried with her were all kinds of artefacts, such as gold sewing needles and weaving tools and jewellery. There were also weapons, such as war clubs. This remarkable discovery shed new light on the mysterious Moche people, who lived in northern Peru from about AD 100 to about 800. Often, these finds raise new questions. Who was the dead woman? She must have been important to have been buried with so many treasures. But why would a woman have been buried with war weapons? Might she have been a queen? Or even a warrior?

Both these important women might have disappeared from history without the work of the archaeologists who found them. Historians then work with the evidence the archaeologists find to piece together the story of the past.

MYSTERY HUNTER

Based on the information you have read, what role do you think the woman found in the Moche grave had in that society? What do the grave objects tell us about the Moche people? You could try to find out more about the pyramid where she was found, called Huaca Cao Viejo.

Chapter 2
LOST KINGDOMS OF AFRICA

Africa is the second biggest continent on the planet, yet we know less about the lost kingdoms of this great continent than about almost anywhere else on Earth. The kingdoms of Africa left few written records, and they vanished long ago. How can we find out about them, and piece together what life was like for their people? Fortunately, there are clues to these mysterious **cultures** in the objects they left behind, in the ruins of their buildings and in the stories and traditions that still survive in Africa today.

Many kingdoms

Hundreds of years ago, Africa was a continent of many kingdoms. Most of them were small, but some of them became so powerful that they conquered their neighbours. These grew into large empires. Some parts of Africa were easier to live in than others. The great Sahara Desert in North Africa was not very inhabited, though people crossed it to trade. Many people lived around Africa's coast and in the region just to the south of the Sahara, called the Sahel. In central Africa, large areas were overgrown with tropical forests. West Africa, however, was a well-**populated** region, and it was here that some of the largest empires rose and fell.

This is the only Almoravid building still standing in Morocco, North Africa.

Power of salt and gold

The first West African empire was called Ghana. It covered a huge area, more than 260,000 square kilometres. This was a trading kingdom. Between about AD 300 and 1200, Ghana controlled the valuable trade in gold and salt in the region. Ghana traded with the Almoravids, a Muslim empire in North Africa that became very powerful in the eleventh century. But as Almoravid power grew in North and West Africa, Ghana's shrank. Eventually, the kingdom fell apart.

This Nok sculpture showing a man resting his chin on his knee was made in Nigeria between 1,700 and 2,500 years ago.

MYSTERIOUS FACTS

Many African kingdoms have risen and fallen:

- The Nok people lived in northern Nigeria, West Africa, between 1000 BC and AD 300, then vanished. They made beautiful clay sculptures, and were early users of iron tools.

- The Bunyoro kingdom was one of the most powerful kingdoms in Central and East Africa from the thirteenth to nineteenth centuries. But Bunyoro was challenged by the rise of its neighbour, Buganda, and the arrival of the British.

The kingdom of Nubia

The first civilization to appear in North Africa is shrouded in mystery. This was not the ancient Egyptians, about whom we know so much, but the Nubians. The kingdom of Nubia seems to have dominated northeastern Africa for thousands of years. It was located along the River Nile to the south of Egypt, and it emerged in about 3000 BC. It is also known as the kingdom of Kush. The Nubians built magnificent cities, such as Napata in the north and Meroe in the south. They have left us some spectacular monuments to remind us of their wealth and power.

Pyramid kings

Nubian kings were powerful rulers, and were buried in elaborate pyramid tombs. Some of the tombs have survived, and give us valuable clues to this lost civilization. Carvings inside show the rulers **enthroned**, surrounded by their **subjects**. Artefacts also tell us that the kingdom became very rich, by trading in gold and other goods.

There are more pyramids in Sudan, built by the ancient Nubians, than there are in Egypt.

This ancient Egyptian wall painting shows Nubian soldiers.

In about 1500 BC, Egypt invaded Nubia and for nearly 500 years Egyptians controlled the kingdom. Eventually, the Nubians won back their independence, and they enjoyed 150 years of peace until about 500 BC. It seems they were then invaded by a people from a mysterious kingdom to the east, the kingdom of Aksum.

Traces of Aksum

Legend tells us that the kingdom of Aksum was created by the son of King Solomon of Israel and the Queen of Sheba, in about 400 BC. Aksum was at its height 700 years later, under King Ezana (AD 325–360). This powerful trading nation controlled the shores of the Red Sea. Ships from as far away as India brought in goods, and Aksum **exported** goods from all over Africa to the rest of the world. We know about Aksum's wealth because some of its gold coins have survived.

King Ezana converted to Christianity and made it the official religion of the kingdom. When he died, he was buried in an elaborate underground chamber. This was marked above the ground by a tall stone column, or **obelisk**, covered in carvings of false windows and doors. This column and others like it have survived, giving us precious clues to the mystery of Aksum.

King Ezana's obelisk marked the location of his grave.

Great Zimbabwe

Three thousand kilometres away, and hundreds of years later, in about AD 1000, another great kingdom flourished in southern Africa. This was Zimbabwe, an important trading power. As in Nubia, its most precious resource was gold. This was mined by women in mines deep in the forest, then processed and carried to the coast to be shipped abroad. No one is quite sure, but Zimbabwe may have been at the centre of a great trading network in central and southern Africa. Its people were the Karanga, who were known to be traders and sailors.

At the heart of the kingdom, on a high **plateau**, was a magnificent stone **complex** now known as Great Zimbabwe. The buildings are surrounded by a huge enclosing wall, 11 metres high. One of the enclosures inside was possibly for the king. A lot of gold and **ceremonial** axes have been found here, suggesting it was an important place. What was it used for? Could Great Zimbabwe have been a religious centre? Or was it just a powerful trading city?

Was this enclosure at Great Zimbabwe used by the king?

What happened?

Historians are not sure quite what happened to the people of Great Zimbabwe, and why their kingdom died out. Perhaps **drought** dried out the land on which their cattle grazed, so they could not feed themselves. Perhaps they moved away because their trading work took them to newer, more important locations. For whatever reason, by AD 1500 the site of Great Zimbabwe was abandoned and the magnificent monument began to fall into ruins.

The obas of Benin

The kingdom of Benin grew in West Africa in the tenth century, among the Edo people. By the fifteenth century, it had become a very wealthy empire. Its ruler was called the oba, and the obas lived in elaborate palaces. Trade continued to make the Benin successful for several hundred years. Merchants even came from Europe to trade with them. From the seventeenth century, however, groups within the empire were fighting each other, making it weaker. When the British took control of the area in the late nineteenth century, the Benin empire came to an end.

The Benin people are famous for the beautiful heads they made in bronze, like this one of an oba. The obas were treated like gods by the people.

MYSTERY HUNTER

Considering the information you have read, why do you think these African kingdoms died out? Was it usually invasion that caused their end, did their people choose to move or were there other factors? Give reasons for your answers.

Chapter 3
LOST KINGDOMS OF THE AMERICAS

The first people arrived in the Americas between 40,000 and 15,000 years ago. They came on foot, over a **land bridge** from Asia to North America. By 12,000 BC, people had moved south and reached South America. At first, these people lived by hunting animals and searching for plants to eat. When people had settled down to become farmers, they could start to build towns and cities. By 2500 BC, they were farming corn in what is now Mexico. The story of kings and kingdoms could begin.

Stone heads

One day, back in the 1850s, a farmer was clearing land in the Mexican jungle when he saw a huge lump of rock sticking out of the ground. As he dug around it, he realized this was no ordinary rock. It was a giant carved head, 1.8 metres high. Who could have made it, and what was it doing in the jungle?

The Olmec heads were carved more than 2,500 years ago.

Later, archaeologists discovered that the head had been carved by the Olmec people, the first civilization to develop in Central America, in the area historians call **Mesoamerica**. The Olmec culture flourished between about 1400 and 400 BC and it was remarkably advanced. The Olmec were expert farmers, they used writing and mathematics, and they built temples to their gods.

Archaeologists have now found 17 Olmec heads, the largest over 3.3 metres tall. What were they for? The rock they are made of had to be brought from mountains over 160 km away, through dense jungle and across rivers. How did the Olmec transport it? The heads are all different, which suggests they may be portraits of real people. They are shown wearing helmets. Are they warriors or kings? Some archaeologists think the Olmec played a ceremonial ball game, with a hard ball. Is that why these men are wearing helmets? Are they team players that their people wanted to honour and remember?

The Olmec also made clay figures of children.

A mysterious end

The first Olmec city was San Lorenzo, but it was abandoned in about 1200 BC and the city of La Venta took its place. In about 350 BC this, too, was destroyed. But why? What made this successful civilization decline and disappear? The jungle soon grew back over the cities, and all trace of the Olmec was lost for thousands of years.

Tula and the Toltec

Mesoamerica continued to be occupied by people who built up large civilizations. The Teotihuacanos were the great power there for nearly 750 years, until about AD 750. That was when invaders from the north arrived, the Toltec. Much less is known about these people, and their mysterious ruler. We do know they conquered a large area, and were fierce fighters as well as successful farmers. In the 1940s, archaeologists made a fantastic discovery: the remains of their capital city, Tula.

Quetzalcoatl, god or man?

According to legend, the city of Tula was founded by a god called Quetzalcoatl. He was a feathered serpent, and the people worshipped him as the god of the planet Venus, the morning star in the sky. But was this god actually the real ruler of the Toltec, their king and high priest, who was worshipped like a god by his people? In the end, Quetzalcoatl's religious practices led to a conflict that forced him into **exile**.

This carving shows the feathered serpent Quetzalcoatl. But was he a god or an important leader of the Toltec?

The story goes that Quetzalcoatl travelled south, towards the coast. At one place, he sat down and wept when he remembered Tula, his capital. Legend has it that his teardrops can still be seen in the stone where they fell. At the coast, Quetzalcoatl wove snakes together to make a raft. He set out to sea, disappearing into the east. There he ascended into the heavens and became the planet Venus.

This legend may be based on fact. Quetzalcoatl's voyage may be connected to a real invasion of the Yucatán Peninsula, to the east. He may actually have led a group of people there and established a new city, at Chichén Itzá. The ruins of this great city, with a stepped pyramid at its heart, can be visited today. But it may have been a different leader who journeyed to the Yucatán; we will never know for sure. We do know that the Toltec civilization declined in the twelfth century, and Tula was later destroyed by the Aztec, who took over the area.

The massive stone figures on top of the pyramid of Quetzalcoatl in Tula are 4.6 metres tall.

MYSTERIOUS FACTS

Here are some facts we know about the city of Tula:

- At its largest, the city covered about 14 square kilometres and was home to 60,000 people.
- The ruins of Tula include a palace, two ball courts and three temples in the shape of low, stepped pyramids.
- The largest pyramid is dedicated to Quetzalcoatl, the god-king. Statues of warriors stand on top of it.

The Chachapoya

We know a lot about the famous Inca, who created a vast empire in the lands of modern Peru and Chile before the Spanish conquered them in the sixteenth century. We know much less about another group of people who lived in Peru before the Inca took over. These were the Chachapoya, who lived high in the Andes Mountains and were known as the Warriors of the Clouds.

Most of what we know about these mysterious people comes from sources belonging to the Inca or to the Spanish conquerors, who had secondhand information about them. Even the name we know them by was given to them by the Inca: we do not know what they called themselves. The Chachapoya did leave some artefacts for us, however, such as pottery, and some ruins of buildings, such as tombs. From these, historians have tried to piece together a picture of their culture.

At Kuelap, the Chachapoya buried their dead in the thick walls, to keep their souls near to them.

Gran Pajatén

High in the **cloud forests** above the Montecristo River valley in the Andes Mountains sit the fragile ruins of Gran Pajatén. The buildings are covered with carvings of humans, birds and geometric shapes. They were discovered by local people only about 50 years ago. Archaeologists think this place was lived in by the Chachapoya, between about AD 800 and 1500. At Gran Pajatén, the Chachapoya placed their dead in tombs carved to look like people, and stood them upright in caves on the mountainside. At other times, they buried the dead in the walls of their buildings, such as in the fortress at Kuelap. They seem to have believed that the dead carried on living among them, so they wanted them to be seen.

The Chachapoya were finally conquered by the Inca in the late fifteenth century, despite having put up fierce resistance. The Inca apparently remained afraid of them, however, because they thought the souls of these cloud warriors continued to roam the region.

Chachapoya tombs are carved to look like people and stand upright on cliffs.

Tiwanaku

One of the most important sites of the ancient world lies at Tiwanaku, in modern-day Bolivia. It is as important as the Great Pyramid of Egypt, or Stonehenge in Britain, yet we know far less about it and the people who created it. This remarkable place is full of unsolved mysteries.

Place of creation

Tiwanaku is located 19 kilometres from Lake Titicaca, a holy lake that lies at the centre of a powerful legend. In the legend, Tiwanaku was the place of creation itself. The creator god arose from Lake Titicaca and commanded the Sun, Moon and stars to rise. He travelled to Tiwanaku, where he created men and women out of stones and sent them to the four corners of the world, so that human life could begin. Later, the creator god grew unhappy with the world and made a terrible storm, causing floods and darkness that nearly wiped out all humans.

Today, there are still some utterly mysterious ruins at Tiwanaku. They are of structures that seem to have been built to line up with the Sun, the Moon and the stars at key times of year. Could the builders of this place have had a developed knowledge of **astronomy** and mathematics? The ruins are built out of massive blocks of stone, so heavy that no one knows exactly how the builders moved them. The style of the structures is unlike any other building in the region of the past 2,000 years.

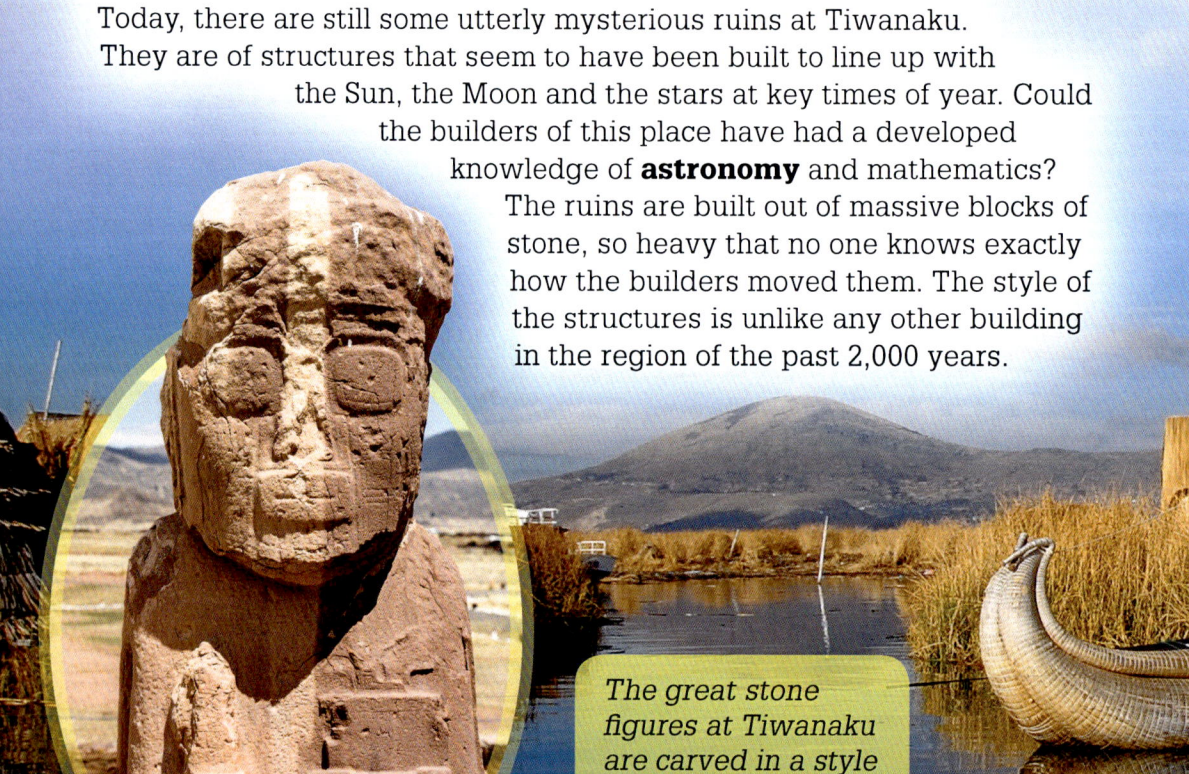

The great stone figures at Tiwanaku are carved in a style unlike others found in the region from later kingdoms.

Truly ancient

Most archaeologists think the structures were built in about AD 500, about 1,500 years ago. But could it be that Tiwanaku is very much older? Some archaeologists have suggested that Tiwanaku could have been built 15,000 to 20,000 years ago, before its people were swept away by a great flood. Modern science agrees that floods swept across this area about 12,000 years ago. There are **myths** of great floods in almost all the ancient cultures of the world, from the same time period. Certainly peoples living in the region many thousands of years later told stories of the founding and use of Tiwanaku, in a time before a great flood.

At Tiwanaku, a sunken temple (in the foreground) leads to Kalasasaya temple (in the background). The statue in the doorway is lit by the Sun at the **equinox**.

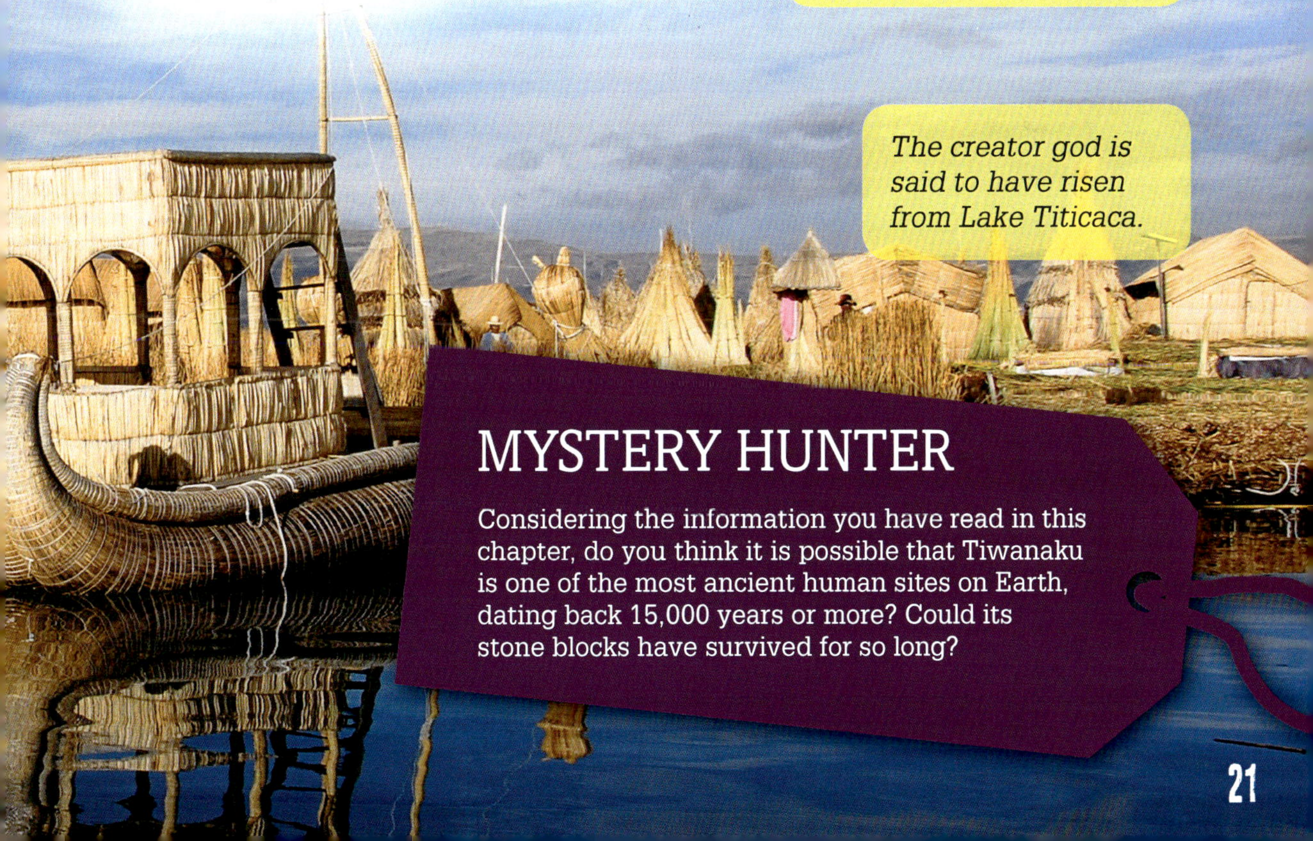

The creator god is said to have risen from Lake Titicaca.

MYSTERY HUNTER

Considering the information you have read in this chapter, do you think it is possible that Tiwanaku is one of the most ancient human sites on Earth, dating back 15,000 years or more? Could its stone blocks have survived for so long?

Chapter 4
GREAT LOST EMPIRES AND THEIR RULERS

Over centuries, empires rise, become powerful, and eventually decline and fall away. The stories of these empires are told for generations afterwards and become part of people's history. Sometimes, we know a lot about these empires, because they leave a lot of evidence behind. At other times, we know much less about them, especially if they left no written records. Occasionally, we come across an empire that seems simply to have vanished, leaving hardly any trace.

Tuwana

One kingdom that became lost in the mists of time is Tuwana. It flourished, in lands that today are in Turkey, during the 800s and 700s BC. We know the kingdom became powerful under a series of kings, but we have details of only a few of them, from inscriptions carved in stone that have been found. Tuwana seems to have become wealthy by controlling trade in the region.

This carving shows King Warpalawas of Tuwana, on the right. He is worshipping the storm god Tarhunzas.

In the end, however, the neighbouring Assyrian empire to the east invaded Tuwana and took over. For thousands of years, Tuwana disappeared from history. Then, in 2012, archaeologists working in Turkey made an exciting discovery: the ruins of a huge city at a site called Kinik Höyük. Could this have been the centre of Tuwana's power? Will archaeologists soon find more evidence to solve the mystery of how these people lived, and how their kingdom came to an end?

Mitanni

A little way further east lay another forgotten kingdom, older than Tuwana, that of the Mitanni. This kingdom existed from about 1500 to 1200 BC, in lands that today are Syria and Iraq. Historians think the culture was heavily influenced by ancient India, but it remains a mystery. Archaeologists are hoping to uncover its capital city, Washukanni, to learn much more about Mitanni. Some archaeologists think the city lies under a mound called Tell Fekheriye in Syria, but other archaeologists disagree.

The beautiful Queen Nefertiti may have been from Mitanni.

MYSTERIOUS FACTS

Some historians believe that Queen Nefertiti (c. 1370–1330 BC), the famous wife of the Egyptian pharaoh Akhenaten, was born in the Mitanni kingdom. The pair may have married to improve relations between the two kingdoms.

Where was Yamatai?

The kingdom of Yamatai in Japan is thought to have existed between about 100 BC and AD 300, but the whole story of this land and its rulers is shrouded in mystery. No one even knows for sure exactly where Yamatai was. The debate over its location has been raging for centuries.

Japan is a country made up of islands. Some people think Yamatai was on the central island of Honshu; others believe it was further south, on Kyushu island. Ancient Japan was called Wa. The oldest records of Japan are accounts written by Chinese travellers in Wa. These are the main source for placing Yamatai on Honshu. Later Japanese histories locate it on Kyushu.

Himiko the priestess-queen

The most famous ruler of this mysterious kingdom is said to have been Queen Himiko. She was not just a queen, but a high priestess, too. People said she had magical powers, which she used to control her kingdom. It is thought that there had been many years of fighting among the ancient kings of Wa, and that the people became so tired of this that they elected Queen Himiko to bring peace. She was the first female ruler, and the kingdom of Yamatai prospered under her rule. There were proper systems of laws and taxation, and trade with neighbouring lands increased, bringing wealth to the kingdom.

Queen Himiko of Yamatai was very popular during her life, and Japanese children today are still taught about her.

For this the people loved Himiko, and they obeyed her commands. They were probably rather fearful of her magical powers, as well!

Unsolved mystery

The records say that Himiko died in AD 248, but the site of her burial is still unknown. If it could be found, it would confirm the location of her kingdom. In 2009, archaeologists thought they might have found it. They found a burial mound in a town called Sakurai, near the ancient capital city of Japan, Nara, in Honshu. Artefacts at the site date from the time of Himiko's death, which fits in with the records. Also, the mound is three times the size of other burial mounds in the region. This suggests that someone important is buried there. However, the Japanese **imperial** family forbade further excavations at the site, so the mystery remains unsolved.

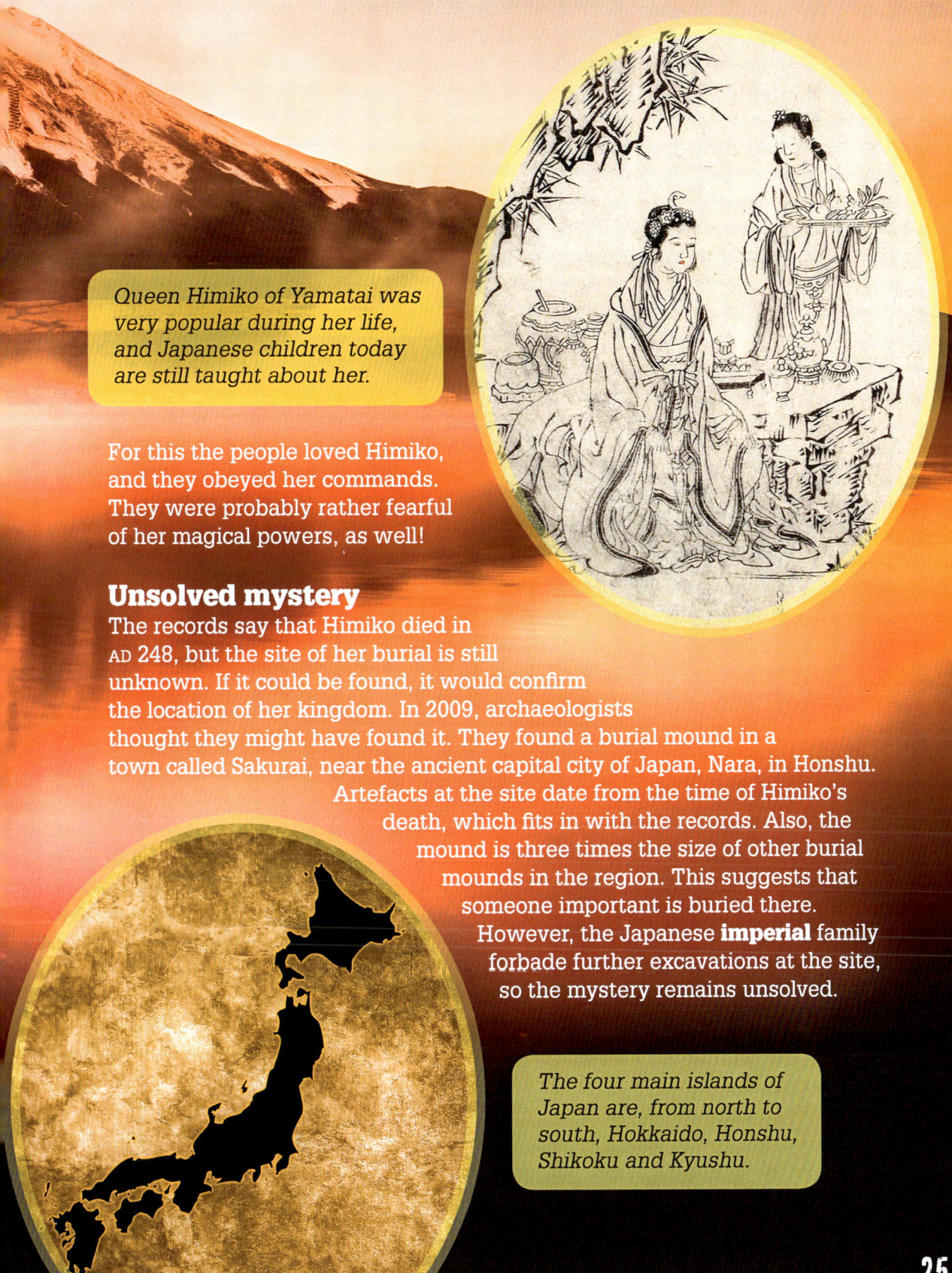

The four main islands of Japan are, from north to south, Hokkaido, Honshu, Shikoku and Kyushu.

Urartu

The lost kingdom of Urartu was in lands that today are Armenia and Turkey, in a mountainous region of western Asia. The Urartu kings took control of the whole region in about 860 BC, and the kingdom flourished for several hundred years until it came to a sudden end in 585 BC. At the time, the kingdom was known as Urartu, but in more modern times it has been known as Van. The mountain we know from the Bible as Mount Ararat was in Urartu, and gave it its name.

A powerful kingdom

The centre of Urartu was its capital, Tushpa. This city was on the shores of Lake Van, which today is in eastern Turkey. This is where the people of Urartu built their remarkable fortress. They had incredible skill in building with stone, which you can still examine there today. Under the rule of King Argishti I (785–753 BC), Urartu was at the height of its power. It had conquered neighbouring lands and was one of the most important kingdoms in the **Middle East**. Argishti I founded several new cities, including Erebuni. He used 6,600 captured slaves to help build it.

The Fortress of Van was built in the ancient kingdom of Urartu during the ninth to seventh centuries BC.

Talented people

As well as being expert builders in stone, the people of Urartu made objects in iron and bronze. They kept written records in an early kind of script called **cuneiform**, in their own Urartian language. Historians have been able to translate these, but another kind of script the Urartu people used, called **hieroglyphics**, remains a complete mystery.

A mysterious end

Despite all this power, Urartu seems to have come to a sudden end in 585 BC. Historians think it was invaded by a people called the Medes, but there is no written record, so we cannot be sure. The archaeology reveals one city that was destroyed by fire, which suggests that the end of the kingdom was swift and violent. Over time, the region became known as Armenia, and the memory of Urartu faded.

This mural shows the Urartian warrior god Khaldi on a lion.

Lake Van is the largest lake in Turkey.

The city of Angkor was covered in stone carvings.

Khmer empire

In southeast Asia, in lands that today are the countries of Cambodia, Thailand, Laos and Vietnam, once stood one of the most remarkable empires in history. This was the Khmer empire. It began in AD 802 and lasted for over 600 years. It was a huge and powerful empire, and boasted some of the most beautiful monuments ever seen.

The city of Angkor

From about 1100, the capital of this vast empire was the city of Angkor. For over a century, Angkor was the largest city in the world. It covered an area as big as modern Los Angeles and was home to up to 1 million people. Its remarkable buildings showed the wealth and power of the empire, its religious devotion and its wonderful art and culture.

Angkor Wat is the largest temple in the world.

In 1113, a king called Suryavarman II (died 1145–1150) came to power in Khmer. The Khmer were Hindus at that time, and Suryavarman wanted to build a magnificent temple in the city of Angkor, to honour the Hindu god Vishnu and to hold his own ashes after his death. This became Angkor Wat, an enormous complex of temple buildings. It is built to face towards the west, because in Hinduism the west represents death. This is why it was also known as the "funeral temple". In the thirteenth century, the Khmer people converted from Hinduism to Buddhism, and the temple was converted for Buddhist use with new statues.

A lost city in the jungle

But where was Khmer's capital city before Angkor? There were inscriptions about a mysterious city called Mahendraparvata, not far from Angkor, but it had never been found. Then, in 2012, scientists used a new technique of scanning the jungle with **lasers** from the air. As the images from the scanner came together, the scientists could hardly believe what they saw. There was a whole city, hidden beneath the jungle! The team travelled to the site to start uncovering the ruins. The city stands on top of a holy mountain, and includes temples, networks of roads and other buildings. Could this be Mahendraparvata? It almost certainly is, and the mystery of Khmer's early capital is finally beginning to be solved.

This statue of the Buddha was added to Angkor Wat when the Khmer people converted from Hinduism to Buddhism.

Persian empire

The Persian empire of western Asia was one of the biggest ever known. Its story is one of great riches and power, but in the end its kings went too far in trying to expand their kingdom, and paid a high price. The empire became weak, and left itself open to attack from outside. One great mystery about the empire remains unsolved, and that is what happened to one of its armies.

A great king

The empire was founded by Cyrus the Great (c. 600/576–530 BC), a Persian king from what is today Iran. In 550 BC, Cyrus joined with his neighbours, the Medes, and proceeded to create the largest empire the world had ever seen. It stretched from the Mediterranean Sea in the west to modern Pakistan in the east, across more than 4,800 km. Cyrus was predominantly a peaceful ruler who allowed the peoples he conquered to continue with their own cultures and religions, as long as they paid taxes and obeyed the law.

The missing army

When Cyrus's son Cambyses II (died 522 BC) became king, he decided to add Egypt to the empire. He sent a huge army into the Egyptian desert – but it was never seen again. Legend says that a great sandstorm blew up and buried them all, but over the centuries, all attempts to find any trace of the army have failed.

In 2009, two Italian archaeologists found a pile of bones and weapons that they claimed was the missing army. But other people say that a sandstorm would not kill an army, and that in any case the soldiers' remains would not be all together in a heap, out in the open. The most likely explanation, they say, is that the army did not disappear at all, but was defeated and captured. The story of the storm was probably invented to stop the shame of the defeat becoming public.

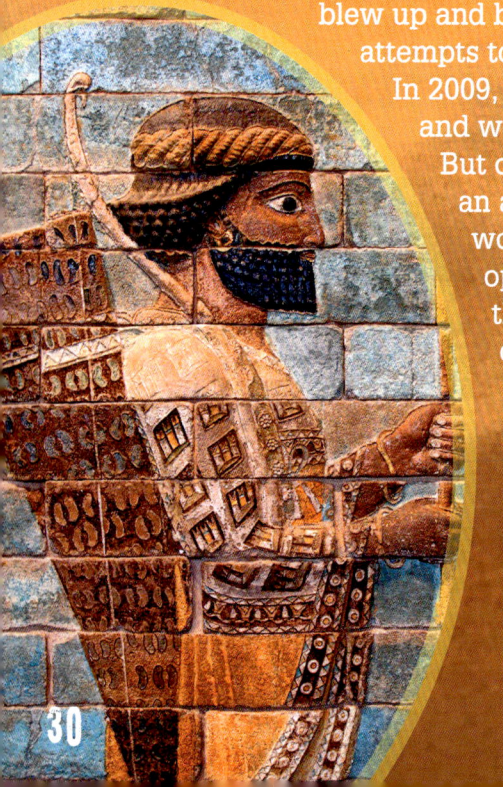

The soldiers of the Persian army were great warriors, but what happened to the army sent by Cambyses II to the Egyptian desert?

The great city of Persepolis was built by order of King Darius. Sculptors were brought from far and wide to create extraordinary carvings.

A step too far

After Cambyses II, Darius I (c. 550–486 BC) became king. He decided to push the empire further west by invading Greece. Darius was defeated, but his son and successor, King Xerxes (518–465 BC), did not learn from this mistake. He, too, attacked Greece, and was again defeated. The Persian empire was never quite the same again, and in 334 BC, Alexander the Great (356–323 BC) of Greece began an attack that ended with him conquering all Persian lands.

MYSTERY HUNTER

Based on the information you have read, what do you think happened to Cambyses II's army in Egypt? Were the soldiers killed by a sandstorm, or was that story invented to hide a defeat? Give reasons for your answer.

Chapter 5
KING ARTHUR

Few kings and kingdoms have captured the imaginations of people so completely, and for so long, as that of King Arthur and his knights. This legendary king is said to have lived in Britain in the late fifth and early six centuries AD, when he led his people, the Britons, against invading Anglo-Saxon tribes from Europe. For over a thousand years, people have been reading stories about King Arthur. Could there be truth in the stories, or is it all just a legend?

Stories of Arthur

The first mention of Arthur comes in *History of the Britons*, which was probably written in AD 830 by a Welsh monk called Nennius. It tells how Arthur led the Britons in battle against the Saxons, but does not call him a king.

It was more than 300 years later that a fuller tale of Arthur appeared, written by Geoffrey of Monmouth (*c.*1100–1155), also a Welshman, in his *History of the Kings of Britain* of 1136. He describes how Arthur was born at a place called Tintagel, was helped by a magician called Merlin, and was married to a beautiful woman called Guinevere. One especially powerful part of the tale said that Arthur proved his right to be king by pulling a magnificent sword, Excalibur, out of a solid block of stone. Merlin had said that only the rightful king would be able to do this.

There is no evidence that the story of Arthur pulling Excalibur from the stone is true.

How much of Monmouth's story was fact and how much was his imagination is not known. The story was a huge hit, and the legend of Arthur took hold in people's imagination.

A romantic tale

In 1152, the King of England, Henry II (1133–1189), married a French bride, Eleanor of Aquitaine, and the stories of Arthur spread to France. French writers developed the legend further, focusing in particular on romantic tales of the love between Arthur and his bride, Guinevere. There was no historical basis to these tales, but they were wonderful to hear.

This romantic photograph of "Lancelot and Guinevere" was taken by the famous nineteenth-century photographer Julia Margaret Cameron (1815–1879).

MYSTERIOUS FACTS

When it comes to King Arthur, it can be hard to distinguish historical fact from myth. But we do know how some myths about the king began:

- In the 1180s, a French writer, Chrétien de Troyes, invented Arthur's friend Sir Lancelot, and the story of his love for Queen Guinevere.

- In the late fifteenth century and sixteenth century, the Tudor kings of England told a story that they were descended from King Arthur, based on no evidence at all.

Arthur's court at Camelot

According to the legend, Arthur lived in a place called Camelot, where he built a castle. There he lived with his queen, Guinevere, and his knights. Together they formed the royal court and debated how to go out and fight for what was right. But where was this mysterious Camelot?

Cadbury or Caerleon?

Cadbury Castle is an old **hill fort** not far from other sites linked to King Arthur in southwest England. The archaeology does show that, around the time Arthur is said to have lived, the fort was strengthened with more defences. There are also signs of a church and a great hall. Certainly the local people have always believed in a magical connection with Arthur and his knights. They say that, if you leave a silver coin with your horse there on Midsummer's Eve, the horse will be found with new horseshoes in the morning.

Tintagel Castle in Cornwall was said to be the place of Arthur's birth. In fact, the ruins date from long after he was supposed to have lived.

Caerleon, on the other hand, is far away to the west in Wales. This fort was suggested by Geoffrey of Monmouth as the place to which Arthur and his soldiers were pushed back by the advancing Anglo-Saxons. Although there are ruins in Carleon, it is just as likely that Geoffrey suggested this place simply because it was close to his own home, and he would have liked the connection to be true.

The Round Table

Wherever Camelot was, the story went that Arthur wanted to prevent fights breaking out between his knights. He did not want them to compete for power. So he arranged that they would hold their meetings around a circular table given to him by Guinevere's father. They became the Knights of the Round Table. The idea of this table, where every person had equal importance, was very appealing, but there is no evidence for it. However, King Henry VIII (1491–1547) was so excited by the idea that, when he came to the throne in 1509, he arranged for an existing round table in Winchester castle to be repainted, with himself at the top like a new King Arthur.

This medieval painting shows Merlin introducing a new knight, Sir Galahad, to the Round Table.

Geoffrey of Monmouth was from Wales, but did Arthur live there?

Arthur's resting place

According to Geoffrey of Monmouth's book *History of the Kings of Britain*, King Arthur was away fighting the Romans in land that today is France, when his wicked nephew, Mordred, seized his throne. Arthur returned to Britain to reclaim his place as king. He killed Mordred in a fierce battle, but he was fatally injured himself.

This painting of Arthur's death was made in 1860, when the story of the legendary king was very popular.

His body was placed in a boat and floated off to the island of Avalon, to rest in peace. His knights threw his precious sword, Excalibur, into the water. The legend also tells us that Arthur never truly died, but that he is waiting until Britain needs his courage and strength once again, when he will return.

A fake tomb?

Where was the isle of Avalon? At the time when Arthur is said to have lived, large areas in the county of Somerset were flooded. A tall hill stood out of the land like an island, at a place called Glastonbury. This came to be linked with the legendary island of Avalon. This is probably why the legend of Arthur says that his body was eventually taken to the **abbey** at Glastonbury, and buried there.

The abbey was destroyed by a fire in 1184. When they were working on the ruins, builders apparently uncovered Arthur's tomb. Was this really the case, or did the monks living in the abbey invent the story so they could attract visitors and raise money to rebuild their church? Some think the tomb at Glastonbury was a fake, but others believe it was genuine.

Was Arthur buried at the abbey in Glastonbury?

Some say Excalibur was thrown into this Welsh lake.

MYSTERY HUNTER

Thinking about what you have read of King Arthur, do you think he was a real king or a legendary figure? Consider our sources for the story of Arthur. How reliable are they? Can you think why the stories might have become so popular with people?

Chapter 6
WHAT HAPPENED TO THEM?

Sometimes a mystery is all about a ruler, rather than his or her kingdom. One of the dangers of having power is that you are likely to make enemies. People who want to take your power for themselves may plot to remove you from the throne or even to kill you. Throughout history, there have been stories of kings and queens, princes and princesses, who have been overthrown. The fates of some of them remain a mystery.

The princes in the tower

One of the greatest mysteries in English history is what happened to two young princes in 1483. They were Prince Edward and his brother, Prince Richard. They were the sons of King Edward IV (1442–1483), and Prince Edward, the elder of the two, had a strong claim to the throne when their father died. However, the boys' uncle, Richard of Gloucester (1452–1485), definitely did not want his nephew to be crowned Edward V. He wanted the crown for himself. In 1483, shortly after their father's death, the two boys were 12 and 9 years old. They were taken to the Tower of London, where they were told they would wait for Edward to be crowned king. In fact, they were held prisoner. The two children were never seen again. What happened to them?

This painting of the Princes in the Tower was made almost 400 years after they died. Their story continued to interest people.

Some people said that Richard of Gloucester, who was soon crowned Richard III, ordered the children to be murdered. Others have said that it was not Richard who ordered the deaths, but Henry VII (1457–1509), who seized the throne after defeating Richard in battle two years later. Henry married the sister of the young princes, and did not want there to be any doubt about his right to rule. Whoever was responsible, the boys had a sad end.

Prince Edward and Prince Richard were held prisoner in the White Tower in the Tower of London.

Could it have been King Henry VII who ordered the murder of the princes in the Tower of London?

MYSTERIOUS FACTS

Do these facts make the story of the lost princes clearer or more mysterious?

- In 1502, a man called Sir James Tyrell confessed to having suffocated the boys with the pillows on their bed. But who ordered him to do it?

- In 1674, workmen discovered the skeletons of two children, buried at the Tower of London. It has never been proven that these are the princes, but the bones were reburied near other kings in London's Westminster Abbey.

King Richard III of England

We will never know whether or not Richard III was responsible for the murder of the two young princes in the Tower of London. But that was not the only mystery surrounding this royal figure.

Wars of the Roses

Richard III was crowned king in 1483. At that time, two families were competing for the throne of England. They were the House of York and the House of Lancaster. The symbol of the Yorks was a white rose, and the symbol of the Lancasters was a red rose, so their struggle was known as the Wars of the Roses. Battles had been going on between the two families since 1455. By the 1480s, the Lancasters were supporting Henry Tudor as their candidate for the throne. Richard belonged to the House of York. Even though he was king, he was still being challenged by Henry Tudor. In 1485, the last great battle in this lengthy war was fought, the Battle of Bosworth, in the county of Leicestershire.

Richard III ruled for only two years, but his death created a gruesome mystery.

By coincidence, Richard's remains were buried under a large "R" that marked a reserved parking space.

The battle was fierce, but Richard and his forces were finally defeated. Richard was killed, and Henry was immediately crowned as the first Tudor king of England. Richard's body was taken to the nearby city of Leicester and buried without ceremony. For hundreds of years, no one knew where he lay. Then, in 2012, archaeologists discovered evidence that the king might lie under a car park in the centre of Leicester. This had once been the location of a church. They dug up the asphalt and found a skeleton. Could this be the missing king?

Science to the rescue

Scientists tested the bones and confirmed they belonged to an adult male who had lived in the late fifteenth century. More importantly, the spine of the skeleton was crooked. Richard was known to have suffered from a deformity in his spine that made him appear hunched. There were also severe injuries to the skull, which had killed the man. The final proof came from **DNA** testing. Scientists traced the direct descendants of Richard III who are living today, and found that their DNA matched that taken from the skeleton. On 12 May 2015, the king was buried in a new tomb in Leicester Cathedral. Finally, he has a grave fit for a king.

Revolution!

In France in 1789, a **revolution** began that changed the course of French history. In the French Revolution, people rose up against the king and the **nobles**. King Louis XVI (1754–1793) and his government were overthrown. In 1793, Louis and his wife, Marie Antoinette, were put to death. What would now happen to their eight-year-old son, Louis? Legally, little Louis was now the king of France. He was kept in prison, and the official record says he died there in 1795. Rumours flew around that he had been murdered, and then that he had escaped. The fate of this child remains a mystery.

This illustration shows the execution of Marie Antoinette, who was killed by the guillotine, a weapon that sliced off heads.

Who was Louis?

One theory was that Louis was taken to America for safety. Dozens of men there later claimed to be Louis. One was Eleazer Williams (1788–1858), a minister in Wisconsin. He had been raised by Mohawks, and claimed he was actually the lost prince. There was no evidence to back up his story.

The candidate with the most convincing story was a German called Karl Wilhelm Naundorff (c. 1785–1845). He convinced the nanny who had looked after Louis, who asked him many questions about his childhood. He said he had been swapped in prison with another child, who died in his place. His claim had wide support. DNA tests carried out in recent decades suggest he was not likely to have been Louis. However, his descendants claim the DNA was not taken from the correct sources.

How can we know the truth?

Some mysteries may never be solved. The job of the mystery hunter is not just to discover the facts about lost kings and kingdoms. The mystery hunter can also question why some stories about kings and kingdoms are passed down through the centuries, but other stories are forgotten. Discovering the answers to these mysteries can tell us not just about the past but about the present and the future.

DNA evidence from a boy's body buried in the Paris prison and from the remains of Marie Antoinette showed a match, suggesting that Louis did in fact die in prison in 1795.

MYSTERY HUNTER

Considering what you have read here, do you think it is likely that Karl Wilhelm Naundorff was actually the lost son of Louis XVI and Marie Antoinette? Give reasons for your answer.

MYSTERY HUNTER ANSWERS

Chapter 1

Q *Based on the information you have read, what role do you think the woman found in the Moche grave had in that society? What do the grave objects tell us about the Moche people? You could try to find out more about the pyramid where she was found, called Huaca Cao Viejo.*

A The woman in the grave must have been important, because she was buried with a rich collection of funeral objects. The fact that weapons were included suggests she might have had some kind of leadership role. From the sewing needles and weaving tools, we learn that Moche people crafted textiles, and from the jewellery that they had metalworking skills.

Chapter 2

Q *Considering the information you have read, why do you think these African kingdoms died out? Was it usually invasion that caused their end, did their people choose to move, or were there other factors? Give reasons for your answers.*

A These kingdoms died out for a variety of different reasons. Benin, for example, came to an end for two reasons. First, its people began to fight among themselves, making the empire weaker. Second, the British arrived and were able to take control of their land. The kingdom of Zimbabwe probably ended when trading conditions changed. Ghana was attacked and overrun from outside, and so was Nubia.

Chapter 3

Q *Considering the information you have read in this chapter, do you think it is possible that Tiwanaku is one of the most ancient human sites on Earth, dating back 15,000 years or more? Could its stone blocks have survived for so long?*

A Myths suggest Tiwanaku is extremely ancient, but this is not necessarily backed up by scientific and historical facts. Most archaeologists date the buildings to only 1,500 years ago. However, the fact that the monument's style does not match other places in the region from 1,500 years ago does open up the possibility that it is older. Its great blocks of hard stone could possibly have survived from 15,000 years ago.

Chapter 4

Q *Based on the information you have read, what do you think happened to Cambyses II's army in Egypt? Were the soldiers killed by a sandstorm, or was that story invented to hide a defeat? Give reasons for your answer.*

A Many people have claimed to find the remains of Cambyses' army, but these claims have been discredited by scientists. It seems more likely that the story of the disastrous storm was invented by Cambyses or his successors to cover up a humiliating defeat.

Chapter 5

Q *Thinking about what you have read of King Arthur, do you think he was a real king, or a legendary figure? Consider our sources for the story of Arthur. How reliable are they? Can you think why the stories might have become so popular with people?*

A There is some evidence that a British warrior leader existed in the fifth and sixth centuries. It is likely that many British leaders defended their lands against the Anglo-Saxon invaders. Apart from that, the story of Arthur is an entertaining invention, created centuries after the period when Arthur may have lived. Perhaps the story of Arthur has remained popular because it is about good defeating evil, and about love.

Chapter 6

Q *Considering what you have read here, do you think it is likely that Karl Wilhelm Naundorff was actually the lost son of Louis XVI and Marie Antoinette? Give reasons for your answer.*

A Naundorff did convince people who had known Louis as a child, but he had no hard proof to back up his claim. The DNA tests suggest he was not Louis, and that the young prince did die in a Paris prison in 1795. However, the tests are disputed by Naundorff's family. This is definitely a mystery that will continue to run.

GLOSSARY

abbey large church where monks live

archaeologists people who study the past by digging for the remains of buildings and objects

artefacts objects from the past

astronomy study of the stars and planets

ceremonial used for religious events

cloud forests tropical mountain forests that are usually covered by low clouds

complex collection of buildings

cultures ways of life of peoples in particular places

cuneiform ancient kind of writing using wedge-shaped marks

decline loss of importance or power

DNA substance in our cells that stores information about our genes. DNA from members of the same family shares characteristics.

drought long period without rain

empires collections of territory ruled by another country

enthroned sitting on a throne

equinox two days each spring and autumn when the day and the night have the same number of hours

evidence objects or information that prove something is true

exile being sent away from your home country

exported goods sent to another country for sale

head of state chief representative of a country

hieroglyphics kind of writing using pictures and symbols

hill fort camp or fortification built on top of a hill for defence

imperial connected with an empire

inscriptions words that are written or carved on a monument

land bridge narrow piece of land connecting two larger landmasses across water

lasers very narrow, intense beams of light

legend old story that may or may not be true

Mesoamerica ancient region in the Americas extending from central Mexico to Belize, Guatemala, El Salvador, Honduras, Nicaragua and northern Costa Rica

Middle East region in western Asia and northeastern Africa

myths old stories, often explaining nature or the early history of humans

nobles high-ranking people in society

obelisk tall column with flat sides

pharaoh ruler of ancient Egypt

plateau area of flat, raised land

populated having people living there

revolution violent and sudden change that overthrows a government

subjects people of a country ruled by a king or queen

FIND OUT MORE

BOOKS

Ancient Egyptians (Analysing Ancient Civilizations), Louise Spilsbury (Raintree, 2019)

Britains Settlement by the Anglo-Saxons and Scots (Early British History), Claire Throp (Raintree, 2016)

Did King Arthur Exist? (Top Secret!), Nick Hunter (Raintree, 2017)

Medieval Knights: Europe's Fearsome Armoured Soldiers (Graphic History: Warriors), Blake Hoena (Raintree, 2020)

WEBSITES

www.dkfindout.com/uk/history/anglo-saxons/anglo-saxon-beliefs/
Find out more about Anglo-Saxon beliefs in Britain, and their impact on modern-day Britain, including our names for the days of the week!

www.natgeokids.com/uk/discover/history/egypt/ten-facts-about-ancient-egypt/
Discover more fascinating facts about ancient Egypt.

INDEX

Aksum kingdom 11
Alexander the Great 31
Almoravid empire 8, 9
ancient Egypt 4, 6, 10, 11, 23, 30
Angkor, Cambodia 5, 28–29
Argishti I 26
Armenia 26, 27
Arthur, king 32–37
Assyrian empire 23
Aztec people 17

Benin empire 13
Buganda kingdom 9
Bunyoro kingdom 9
burial of the dead 7, 10, 11, 18, 19, 25, 36–37, 39, 41, 43

Cambyses II 30–31
Camelot 34
Chachapoya 18–19
Chichén Itzá, Mexico 17
Cyrus the Great 30

Darius I 31
DNA testing 41, 43

Excalibur 32, 36
Ezana, king 11

flood myths 21
French Revolution 42

Ghana empire 9
gold 9, 10, 11, 12
Gran Pajatén, Peru 19
Great Zimbabwe 12–13

Hatshepsut 6
Henry VII (Henry Tudor) 39, 40–41
Henry VIII 35
Himiko, queen 24–25

Inca civilization 18, 19

Japan 24–25

Karanga people 12–13
Khmer empire 28–29
Kuelap, Peru 18, 19

Lake Titicaca 20–21
Louis, prince 42–43
Louis XVI 42

Mahendraparvata, Cambodia 29
Medes people 27
Mesoamerica 14–17
Mitanni kingdom 23
Moche people 7

Nefertiti 23
Nennius 32
Nok culture 9
Nubian kingdom 10–11

obelisks 11
Olmec civilization 14–15

Persian empire 30–31
Peru 7, 18–19
Princes in the Tower 38–39

queens 6, 7, 23, 24–25, 26, 27, 42–43
Quetzalcoatl 16–17

Richard III (of Gloucester) 38–39, 40–41
Round Table 35

Suryavarman II 29

Teotihuacanos people 16
Tintagel 34
Tiwanaku, Bolivia 20–21
Toltec civilization 16–17
Tudor kings 33, 35, 39, 40–41
Tula, Mexico 16–17
Tuwana kingdom 22–23

Urartu kingdom 26–27

Warpalawas, king 22

Yamatai kingdom 24–25

Zimbabwe 12–13